How Does a

David

Rigby®

A Harcourt Achieve Imprint

www.Rigby.com
1-800-531-5015

How does a tree help?
It is a bug's home.

How does a tree help?
It is a raccoon's home.

How does a tree help?
It is a bird's home.

How does a tree help?
It is a snake's home.

How does a tree help?
It is a monkey's home.

How does a tree help?
It is a bear's home.

How does a tree help?

It is my home!